ile: _____ 1100L _____

/BL: _____ 8.9 _____

Points: _____ 2.0 _____

What If We Do NOTHING?

NUCLEAR PROLIFERATION

Joseph Harris

Gareth Stevens
Publishing

Please visit our web site at: www.garethstevens.com.
For a free color catalog describing Gareth Stevens Publishing's list of high-quality books, call 1-800-542-2595 (USA) or 1-800-387-3178 (Canada). Gareth Stevens Publishing's fax: 1-877-542-2596

Library of Congress Cataloging-in-Publication Data

Harris, Joseph, 1982–
   Nuclear proliferation / by Joseph Harris.
     p. cm. – (What if we do nothing?)
   Includes bibliographical references and index.
   ISBN-10: 1-4339-1983-4   ISBN-13: 978-1-4339-1983-1 (lib. bdg.)
   1. Nuclear nonproliferation–Juvenile literature.   2. Nuclear weapons–Juvenile literature.   I. Title.
JZ5675.H37   2010
327.1'747–dc22   2008052285

This North American edition published in 2010 by Gareth Stevens Publishing under license from Arcturus Publishing Limited.
Gareth Stevens Publishing
A Weekly Reader® Company
1 Reader's Digest Road
Pleasantville, NY 10570-7000 USA

Copyright © 2009 Arcturus Publishing Limited
Produced by Arcturus Publishing Limited
26/27 Bickels Yard, 151-153 Bermondsey Street, London SE1 3HA

Series Concept: Alex Woolf
Editor: Alex Woolf
Designer: Phipps Design
Picture Researcher: Alex Woolf

Gareth Stevens Executive Managing Editor: Lisa M. Herrington
Gareth Stevens Editors: Jayne Keedle, Joann Jovinelly
Gareth Stevens Senior Designer: Keith Plechaty

Picture Credits: Corbis: Cover, top right (Dallas and John Heaton/Free Agents Limited), 10 (Bettmann), 14 (Jean-Paul Pelissier/Reuters), 16 (Bettmann), 19 (Abedin Taherkenareh/epa), 20 (Pakistan Military Department/Handout/Reuters), 31 (Bettmann), 33 (Neville Elder/Corbis Sygma), 35 (Reuters), 36 (Reuters), 38 (Reuters); Cover bottom left and 41 (Reuters), 44 (Kimmasa Mayama/epa); Getty Images: 8 (George Silk/Time & Life Pictures), 26 (Scott Peterson), 28 (Arif Ali/AFP), 43 (Digital Globe); PA Photos: 24 (Dennis Cook/AP); Rex Features: 13 (Everett Collection); Corbis (Bettmann): Cover, background and 4 (U.S. Department of Energy), 7 (Roger Harris), 23 (U.S. Department of Energy).

Cover pictures: Bottom left: A South Korean protester burns North Korea's national flag beside mock nuclear missiles during an anti-North Korea protest in Seoul, South Korea, on August 15, 2003. Top right: The Atomic Bomb Memorial Dome in Hiroshima, Japan. Background: A mushroom cloud is produced by the detonation of a 10.4-megaton nuclear bomb. The test was carried out by the United States on Elugelab, an island in the Eniwetok Atoll, a part of the Pacific Island chain, on November 1, 1952.

Every attempt has been made to clear copyright. Should there be any inadvertent omission, please apply to the publisher for rectification.

Printed in the United States

1 2 3 4 5 6 7 8 9 15 14 13 12 11 10 09

Contents

CHAPTER 1

The Power of Atoms

It is 2025. Min-sik is a very worried young man. The dictator of a neighboring state possesses nuclear weapons and is threatening to attack the Southeast Asian country where Min-sik lives. The dictator has issued many such threats since he acquired nuclear weapons. Until now, fear of retaliation by other nuclear-armed countries has stopped him from carrying them out. However, the dictator is erratic and there is no guarantee that he will be dissuaded this time. Min-sik has read books about the devastating effects of nuclear weapons. He knows that many thousands of people will die in a nuclear blast and that the radioactive fallout from the explosion will pollute the environment over a wide area. He wishes he could be free from the constant fear of nuclear attack.

Nuclear Bombs

Nuclear weapons are the most devastating weapons ever invented. A nuclear device produces an explosion far more powerful than any other kind of bomb. Because of their awesome power, people often refer to nuclear weapons simply as "the Bomb." As well as possessing enormous destructive force, nuclear weapons also leave behind harmful radioactive dust called fallout.

A nuclear explosion sends large amounts of hot gas, dust, and debris into the air above a test site in Nevada. The result is a unique shape in the sky, usually described as a mushroom cloud. The mushroom cloud became the symbol of the nuclear age and the threat of a terribly destructive war.

THE POWER OF BOMBS

This chart shows the estimated numbers killed in some bomb attacks on civilian targets during World War II, and the tonnage of bombs used. The incredible power of nuclear weapons, compared with other types of bombs, is clear.

Date	Location	Type of bombs	Tonnage of bombs	Numbers killed
September 7, 1940 to May 11, 1941	London and other U.K. cities (WWII's "Blitz")	Explosives and incendiaries	18,000	40,000–43,000
May 30, 1942	Cologne, Germany	Explosives and incendiaries	1,455	450–500
July 28, 1943	Hamburg, Germany	Explosives and incendiaries	2,313	30,000–40,000
February 14-15, 1945	Dresden, Germany	Explosives and incendiaries	2,660	30,000–35,000
August 6, 1945	Hiroshima, Japan	Nuclear (uranium)	4	90,000–140,000
August 9, 1945	Nagasaki, Japan	Nuclear (plutonium)	4.5	60,000–80,000

Sources: www.historyplace.com/worldwar2/timeline/ww2time.htm; Royal Air Force - www.raf.mod.uk/bombercommand/thousands.html; Air Force Historical Studies Office - www.airforcehistory.hq.af.mil/PopTopics/dresden.htm; www.historylearningsite.co.uk/hamburg_bombing_1943.htm; Radiation Effects Research Foundation: www.rerf.or.jp/general/qa_e/qa1.html

One nuclear explosion can destroy an entire city. A large number could ruin Earth's environment and climate, producing a nuclear winter in which the planet would cool and many species would become extinct. An all-out nuclear war could destroy human civilization and perhaps all life on Earth. The impact of nuclear weapons is so horrific that no sane person wants to see them used, and many people would like them completely dismantled.

Since the United States manufactured the first nuclear weapon in 1945, huge numbers have been produced. Today, nine countries have nuclear weapons. Between them they possess thousands of bombs. The spread of nuclear weapons to different countries is called nuclear proliferation. The more those weapons proliferate, the greater the danger of a nuclear war.

Scientific Breakthrough

Twentieth-century scientific discoveries led to the creation of nuclear bombs. The great physicist Albert Einstein showed that mass, which is matter or physical substance, could be transformed into energy, the driving force that makes things happen. Once that was understood, scientists began practical experiments to convert mass into energy.

Nuclear Energy

In order to release energy, scientists had to split apart the building blocks of matter, which are called atoms. Scientists once believed that atoms were the smallest things in the universe. They later discovered even smaller units, called particles. At the center of every atom there is a cluster of particles known as its nucleus. Splitting the nucleus of an atom proved to be the key to releasing some of its mass as energy. That is how nuclear energy got its name. Its power comes from the nucleus of an atom, so it is called nuclear or atomic energy. Scientists use the word fission for splitting, so nuclear (or atomic) fission describes the process that creates nuclear energy.

ALBERT EINSTEIN
Albert Einstein (1879–1955) was among the most famous scientists of the 1900s. Born in Germany, he made his most important discoveries while working in the Swiss Patent Office in Bern. His Special Theory of Relativity, published in 1905, proved that matter and energy were related. A famous equation, $E = mc^2$, shows that a small mass can become a large amount of energy, since the potential energy of a mass *(E)* is calculated by multiplying the mass *(m)* by the speed of light *(c)* squared. Light travels at 186,282 miles per second (299,792,458 meters per second), so the speed of light squared is an extremely high number. That is why relatively small amounts of nuclear fuel can produce enormous explosions.

Nuclear power does not have to be used solely for weapons. Nowadays nuclear power stations produce electricity that powers homes, offices, and factories. However, nuclear power and nuclear weapons use similar technology. The radioactive fuel and waste used in power stations can be modified for use in weapons. That means that some countries or groups might try to use civilian nuclear power programs as a front for developing nuclear weapons.

The Manhattan Project

In August 1939, Einstein wrote a letter to U.S. President Franklin Delano Roosevelt. He suggested that it was possible to use atomic

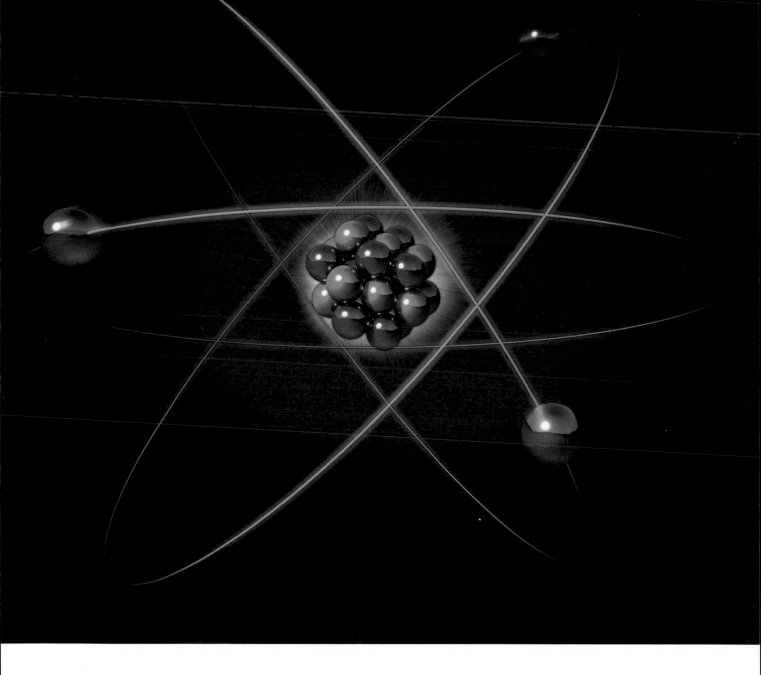

fission to create a weapon of unprecedented power. The aggressive Nazi regime in Germany was on the march, and Einstein was worried that German scientists might master the technology first. Roosevelt ordered research into Einstein's theories immediately. Soon after, World War II (1939–1945) broke out.

That research intensified after the United States entered the war in December 1941. Huge resources were poured into a new initiative, the Manhattan Project, based at Los Alamos, New Mexico. It involved thousands of people and multiple sites, and cost nearly $2 billion.

This image represents a single atom of matter. Each of the colored spheres is a subatomic particle. The central cluster of green and red particles is the nucleus of the atom.

7

The scientists' objective was to create a fission chain reaction. That meant that when an atom was split, the particles given off would split the nuclei of other atoms, which would split still others, and so on. The chain reaction could only be achieved by using isotopes, which are rare forms of radioactive materials such as uranium and plutonium. Radioactive materials emit energy in the form of streams of particles as their unstable atoms decay.

On July 16, 1945, after three years of research, scientists working on the Manhattan Project succeeded in creating a fission chain reaction in a mass of plutonium. A test in the desert, code-named Trinity, produced the world's first nuclear detonation. The explosion had a force equivalent to 19 kilotons (19,000 tons of TNT) and lit up the sky over New Mexico. An enormous ball of fire shot upward,

The Japanese city of Hiroshima was devastated by the atomic bomb dropped by U.S. forces on August 6, 1945. The nuclear shock wave flattened most of the city, leaving only a few strongly constructed buildings standing.

crowned by a mushroom-shaped plume of vapor and debris. Some of the scientists, including the head of the project, J. Robert Oppenheimer, were appalled by the destructive power of the new weapon they had created.

Hiroshima and Nagasaki

Soon afterward, the United States used nuclear bombs for the first time as weapons of war. Between 1941 and 1945, the United States had been waging war against Japan in the Pacific Ocean. By 1945, the United States was on the verge of victory, but Japan refused to surrender. It seemed as though the United States would have to invade mainland Japan to end the war. Such an invasion would likely cost the lives of many thousands of soldiers and civilians. The U.S. government decided instead to use its nuclear bombs on two Japanese cities to persuade the Japanese government to surrender.

On August 6, 1945, a nuclear bomb, code-named "Little Boy," was dropped on the city of Hiroshima. The bomb's core was made up of uranium, and it had an explosive force of 20 kilotons. The blast instantly killed thousands. Many who survived the explosion suffered horrific injuries and died slow, painful deaths later. Two-thirds of the city was leveled and much of the rest was set on fire. Three days later, a 22-kiloton plutonium bomb, code-named "Fat Man," was dropped on Nagasaki. Japan surrendered within a few days.

Those have been the only times nuclear weapons have been used in war. However, the destruction of the two cities provided a chilling demonstration of what nuclear weapons could do. The proliferation of such weapons has come to be recognized as one of the great problems of the modern age.

WHAT WOULD YOU DO?

You Are in Charge

You represent the U.S. Department of Defense at a debate about the ethics of nuclear weapons. The topic of discussion is whether your country should keep or dispose of its nuclear weapons. What do you think?

■ We should get rid of our nuclear weapons, regardless of what other nations do. We must set an example.

■ We *might* get rid of our nuclear weapons, but only if other nations agree to do the same.

■ We should keep our nuclear weapons; we might need them to defend ourselves or to deter others from attacking us.

CHAPTER 2

The Nuclear Arms Race

It is 2025. Nina lives in a small mountain village. She spends most of her time in the fields, looking after the crops. Nina's parents tell her that life was once much easier and more pleasant, but that years earlier a nuclear war badly damaged the planet. Radioactive dust from nuclear explosions has clouded the atmosphere, making it hard for the Sun's rays to get through. That has caused a catastrophic drop in temperature. Nina's country used to have warm summers and mild winters. Now the winters are so cold that nothing can be grown for months. The village faces a constant struggle to harvest enough food to survive. Other settlements are equally poor and isolated from one another.

The Cold War

After World War II ended in 1945, a bitter rivalry developed between the world's two superpowers, the United States and the Soviet Union. The Soviet Union, or U.S.S.R., was a communist state, centered on present-day Russia. Many of the world's nations allied themselves with one or the other of the superpowers. The democracies of Western Europe backed the United States, while most of Eastern Europe became part of the communist

Ethel and Julius Rosenberg leave U.S. Federal Court in New York City. The Rosenbergs were tried and convicted of passing on atomic secrets to the Soviet Union. They were executed on June 19, 1953. They were the only civilians to be executed for spying during the Cold War.

alliance. That division of the world into two armed camps dominated international politics for more than 40 years. That period is known as the Cold War. The rivalry was often intensely hostile and threatening but it never led to an actual war between the superpowers. The Cold War lasted until the early 1990s, when the Soviet Union collapsed.

The Soviets successfully tested a nuclear bomb in 1949, ending the U.S. nuclear monopoly. That led to the first nuclear proliferation as the superpowers competed for dominance. People lived with the possibility of a war in which both sides might use nuclear weapons.

GLOBAL STOCKPILES OF NUCLEAR WEAPONS

This table shows the numbers of weapons possessed by each of the five nuclear powers during the Cold War.

	United States	Soviet Union	United Kingdom	France	China
1945	6	0	0	0	0
1950	369	5	0	0	0
1955	3,057	200	10	0	0
1960	20,434	1,605	30	0	0
1965	31,642	6,129	310	32	5
1970	26,119	11,643	280	36	75
1975	27,052	19,055	350	188	185
1980	23,764	30,062	350	250	280
1985	23,135	39,197	300	360	425
1990	21,211	33,417	300	505	430
1995	10,953	14,978*	300	500	400

*This figure refers to operational warheads possessed by Russia after the fall of the Soviet Union.

Source: Natural Resources Defense Council – www.nrdc.org/nuclear/nudb/datab19.asp

The H-Bomb

The first nuclear weapons were called A-bombs, short for atomic bombs. In 1952, the United States tested a new and more devastating form of nuclear weapon, the H-bomb, or hydrogen bomb. It worked on a similar principle to the A-bomb but the nuclear chain reaction took place in a different way.

Atomic bombs were based on nuclear *fission*. Atoms of nuclear fuel were broken apart to produce a chain reaction that releases enormous amounts of energy. The H-bomb was based on nuclear *fusion*. Instead of being broken apart, atoms were forced to fuse together. For this reason, H-bombs are also known as fusion bombs, or thermonuclear bombs. H-bombs produced a vast explosive yield. America's first H-bomb had a powerful force of 7 megatons (7 million tons of TNT). It was tested on a small island in the South Pacific. Its detonation was so powerful that the island was wiped off the face of Earth.

The Soviet Union soon matched the United States' success. In 1953, it tested a hybrid bomb, using elements of fusion technology. It followed this in 1955 with the detonation of a true H-bomb. Each side was now capable of deploying weapons 350 times more powerful than the bombs dropped on Hiroshima and Nagasaki.

Deterrence

Each superpower began to stockpile weapons in order to gain an advantage over the enemy. The nuclear arms race had begun. The United States had a head start but the Soviet Union made astonishingly rapid progress.

A strategy soon evolved known as deterrence. Deterrence was based on the

THE CUBAN MISSILE CRISIS

In 1962, the nightmare of nuclear war seemed about to become a reality. The Soviet Union was secretly planning to install nuclear missiles on the territory of its ally Cuba, an island just 90 miles (145 kilometers) from the U.S. coast. In October 1962, the Americans discovered the Soviet plan. President John F. Kennedy ordered the U.S. Navy to blockade Cuba and prevent Soviet ships from delivering nuclear missiles. For a few days the world held its breath. If the Soviet ships resisted the blockade, war might develop. Fortunately, both Kennedy and the Soviet leader, Nikita Khrushchev, realized how serious the situation was and managed to come to an agreement. The Soviet Union agreed to remove its missiles from Cuba. In return, the United States guaranteed that it would not invade the island and secretly promised to remove its nuclear weapons from Turkey. Deterrence won the day.

idea that a nation would threaten immense retaliation if attacked. People hoped that threat would deter, or prevent, an enemy attack.

As each superpower's arsenals grew, it soon became apparent that any nuclear exchange would mean mutually assured destruction (MAD). An attack by either side would result in the certain destruction of both. British statesman Winston Churchill famously described the situation as a "balance of terror."

The Cold War was depicted in the 1964 comedy, *Dr. Strangelove*. In the movie, a trigger-happy U.S. General, Buck Turgidson, played by George C. Scott (*left*), tries to persuade the U.S. president to launch a nuclear attack on the Soviet Union.

French soldiers take part in a training exercise. They are practicing the procedures for dealing with a nuclear accident in which radioactive material has leaked from a nuclear weapon. They are wearing protective decontamination suits and carry equipment to scan for radiation.

By the 1960s, the United States and the Soviet Union both possessed arsenals of H-bombs. New technology meant that those could be delivered to targets around the world via aircraft, submarines, and intercontinental ballistic missiles (ICBMs). ICBMs are powerful rockets that can carry nuclear warheads across vast distances.

Policymakers on both sides of the Cold War divide came to believe that a nuclear war could not be won. Even a surprise attack, or first strike, would not prevent the enemy from delivering an equally devastating second strike. Radar could identify the incoming missiles and the nation under attack would be able to retaliate, or strike back, before the missiles arrived. Moreover, both sides had nuclear-armed submarines and aircraft in different parts of world, ready to carry out a nuclear strike at short notice.

Cold War Proliferation

The growing arsenals of the United States and the Soviet Union were not the only concern. Three other nations involved in the Cold War became independent

NUCLEAR ACCIDENTS

The nuclear arms race threatened the world with war, but it also created fears that a catastrophic accident might occur. Nuclear weapons contain conventional explosives as part of their trigger mechanisms. If those are set off accidentally, through human or mechanical error, they would probably not cause a full-scale nuclear detonation. However, harmful radioactive material from the bomb might spread over a wide area. In 1956, there was a near disaster at the Royal Air Force (RAF) base at Lakenheath in Suffolk, England. A B-47 bomber crashed into a storage facility containing nuclear weapons and set it on fire. Fortunately, the blaze was put out and the explosives in the nuclear weapons failed to detonate. Some experts believe that even if nuclear war is avoided, the spread of nuclear weapons will sooner or later lead to an accidental disaster.

nuclear powers — Britain in 1952, France in 1960, and China in 1964. At the time, however, the spread of nuclear weapons to other countries seemed less important than doing something about the expanding arsenals of the superpowers, which dwarfed those of their allies. Political leaders focused their energies on trying to end the superpower arms race and even to achieve some level of disarmament.

Test Ban Treaty

At various times, both sides in the Cold War made efforts to limit the arms race. One obvious way of doing that was to ban the testing of nuclear bombs, which polluted the atmosphere and made it easier to develop new and more powerful weapons. International talks on the subject succeeded up to a point. However, there was no way to know for sure whether a country was conducting secret underground tests. So instead of an absolute ban, a Partial Test Ban Treaty was signed on July 25, 1963 that forbade tests in Earth's atmosphere, underwater, and in outer space.

NUCLEAR TESTS

This chart shows the estimated number of nuclear tests, by nation, carried out between 1945 and 2006.

Nation	Number of tests
United States	1,030
Soviet Union/Russia	715
France	210
China	45
United Kingdom	45
India	4
Pakistan	2
North Korea	1

Source: Natural Resources Defense Council - www.nrdc.org/nuclear/nudb/datab15.asp

SALT I and II

The superpowers' arsenals grew at a fearful rate during the Cold War. Leaders on both sides recognized that development as dangerous, but talks on disarmament usually stalled. The main reason for that was that neither side trusted the other to carry out any agreed reductions. However, in 1969, the United States and the Soviet Union began serious discussions about reducing their strategic (long-range) nuclear weapons. The first round of talks, known as SALT I (Strategic Arms Limitation Treaty), produced an agreement to limit the growth of strategic arsenals. SALT I was signed by both nations in 1972. A second round of talks, known as SALT II, dragged on throughout the 1970s. It was finally signed in 1979 but was short lived. In 1986, U.S. President Ronald Reagan withdrew from the agreement over alleged Soviet violations.

ABM Treaty

The SALT I talks also led to the Anti-Ballistic Missile (ABM) Treaty, signed in 1972. That agreement placed limits on the use of anti-ballistic missile systems. Those are missile defense systems designed to shoot down enemy nuclear missiles. A defensive system is useful, but it encourages the development of new, smarter nuclear missiles, capable of penetrating the ABM shield. Furthermore, if one nation believes that it is protected from the other's missiles, it might be tempted to launch a nuclear attack. Those were some of the reasons

Former U.S. President Ronald Reagan (*left*) meets with then Soviet leader Mikhail Gorbachev. In the 1980s, the two leaders managed to negotiate major reductions in the nuclear arsenals of both nations. Here they sign a 1987 treaty to eliminate their countries' intermediate-range nuclear missiles.

why both the United States and the Soviet Union signed the treaty, which restricted each of them to only two ABM sites.

START I and II

From 1982, the United States and Soviet Union engaged in further negotiations to reduce their nuclear arsenals. START I, the Strategic Arms Reduction Treaty, was signed in 1991. However, the collapse of the Soviet Union delayed it from being carried out. The treaty was finally implemented and went into force in 2001. It resulted in the destruction of about 80 percent of all strategic nuclear weapons then in existence. A second arms reduction treaty, START II, was signed by the United States and Russia in 1993, but was never implemented.

By the mid-1990s, the arsenals of the two major nuclear powers had become less of an issue. World leaders turned their attention to the spread of nuclear weapons to other nations.

WHAT WOULD YOU DO?

You Are in Charge

You are a diplomat from a country that is attempting to develop nuclear weapons. Your nation's main enemy already has them. You meet with representatives of the international community who want you to end your nuclear program. How do you defend your government's decision to continue its nuclear weapons program? Why?

- Your country needs nuclear weapons if it is to have any chance in a conflict with its nuclear-armed enemy.

- Countries that have nuclear weapons have no right to tell other nations that they cannot develop them.

- Having nuclear weapons will prevent war. Your country and its enemy would not dare go to war when both might be destroyed in a nuclear exchange.

CHAPTER 3

Tackling Nuclear Proliferation

It is 2025. Ariel lives in Tel Aviv, the second largest city in Israel. Because it is a small state surrounded by hostile neighbors, Israel has long been prepared against attacks. When Ariel is older, he will have to serve in Israel's army. But Ariel's immediate future is threatened. Israel has had its own nuclear weapons for many years. But now a nearby state, committed to the destruction of Israel, has also become a nuclear power. Israel would probably be able to retaliate against a nuclear attack with a devastating second strike. But feelings in the region are so conflicted that Ariel is not sure that the prospect of retaliation will be enough to deter a nuclear attack. He thinks that Israel may even use its nuclear bombs first to destroy the enemy weapons before they can be used. Ariel is angry that the international community did not do more to prevent Israel's neighbor from acquiring nuclear weapons.

The Nuclear Non-Proliferation Treaty

During the late 1960s, the international community began to recognize that the world would be safer if no more countries acquired nuclear weapons. The more nuclear weapons spread around the world, the greater the risk of their accidental or deliberate use. That concern led to the creation of a Nuclear Non-Proliferation Treaty (NPT) in 1968. The treaty came into force in 1970.

Countries that did not have nuclear weapons signed the treaty pledging not to develop them. However, they were permitted to use nuclear energy for peaceful purposes in power plants. As part of the treaty, nations with nuclear technology promised to help others build nuclear power stations to provide electricity. The five nuclear-armed states — the United States, the Soviet Union, Britain, France, and China — agreed not to help other nations develop nuclear weapons.

The treaty was backed by inspections carried out by the International Atomic Energy Agency (IAEA), which operates as part of the United Nations (U.N.). Its inspectors have access to the civilian nuclear power programs of the countries without nuclear weapons that signed the treaty. Their job was to ensure that nuclear weapons were not being developed. By the 2000s, 189 nations had signed the treaty.

Inspectors from the International Atomic Energy Agency look over an Iranian uranium production facility. Iran allowed the 2007 visit in an effort to convince the world that it was not developing nuclear weapons.

THE INTERNATIONAL ATOMIC ENERGY AGENCY

The International Atomic Energy Agency (IAEA) is an international organization linked with the United Nations. It was set up in 1957 to promote peaceful uses of nuclear technology. It advises countries on safety procedures, helping them use the technology without endangering their populations. The IAEA also has special safeguard agreements with more than 145 nations around the world. The agency inspects the civilian nuclear programs of countries that have signed the NPT and do not have nuclear weapons. In this way, the IAEA can check that nuclear material is not being used to manufacture weapons. In 2005, the agency and its director general, Mohamed ElBaradei, were awarded the Nobel Peace Prize.

Proliferation in the NPT Era

The NPT came into force in 1970 but its existence has not prevented the proliferation of nuclear weapons. India, Israel, and Pakistan refused to sign the treaty and developed their own weapons programs. Israel has never admitted to possessing nuclear weapons. However, experts believe it developed them sometime in the 1960s. As far as is known, Israel has not tested its nuclear weapons.

Successful nuclear tests were carried out by India in 1974 and by Pakistan in 1998. The fact that India and Pakistan both possess nuclear weapons is of particular concern. Those countries have fought each other on several occasions and relations between them remain fragile. That example demonstrates a way in which nuclear weapons can spread, with one and then the other of two rival powers seeking security or advantage by acquiring nuclear weapons.

The nuclear-armed members of the NPT, including the United States and Russia, have not helped the situation by failing to live up to their obligations under the treaty. While criticizing any nation that wishes to develop nuclear weapons, they have continued to develop their own ever more powerful weapons systems. That has certainly weakened their arguments and damaged the goals of non-proliferation.

The End of the Cold War

In the 1990s, the Soviet Union collapsed and broke up into a number of independent states. The Cold War ended. The superpower rivalry had been, until that time, the driving

Pakistan tests a medium-range Ghauri missile carrying a nuclear warhead. With a range of up to 932 miles (1,500 km), those missiles can strike at major targets within India.

force behind the buildup of nuclear weapons. Therefore, many people thought that disarmament would rapidly follow. However, the world's arsenals did not disappear. Russia, the dominant state from the former Soviet Union, was determined to maintain its status as a major nuclear power. Weapons also remained stationed in the newly independent former Soviet republics, Belarus, Kazakhstan, and Ukraine.

Meanwhile, new threats emerged in other parts of the world. Countries, including Iraq and Iran, became ambitious to acquire nuclear weapons. At the same time, terrorism became a global menace. Many people feared that dictators or terrorists might obtain the materials needed to manufacture nuclear weapons. The Cold War period, with its balance of terror, gave way to a different, more insecure, world.

WHAT WOULD YOU DO?

You Are in Charge

You belong to a group that is opposed to nuclear weapons and hope to see them dismantled. Your group is divided over the issue of nuclear power. Some members want to see nuclear power stations shut down, while others only want nuclear weapons outlawed. Which side will you join, and how will you justify your choice?

■ You think that your group should campaign against nuclear power as well as nuclear weapons. You argue that nuclear power production can be used as a first step to producing weapons technology.

■ You think that your group should oppose nuclear weapons. You believe that nuclear power may be needed to meet the energy needs of the future as fossil fuels such as oil and coal grow increasingly scarce.

CHAPTER 4

The Nuclear Black Market

It is 2025. A nuclear weapon has been stolen from the facility where Petri works as a security guard. His country possesses a large number of nuclear weapons. But times are hard and the economy is in crisis. Political leaders are more concerned with maintaining the supply of basic goods than with safeguarding the nuclear arsenal. The storage facility is very large and only a few guards patrol it at any one time. There is no high-tech equipment to protect the nuclear weapons, just fences, barbed wire, and padlocks. To make matters worse, Petri and his colleagues have not been paid for several weeks. He suspects another guard may have helped the robbers. Petri dreads to think what sort of people would want to steal a nuclear missile, and what they might do with it.

Building a Nuclear Bomb

The information required to build a nuclear weapon is readily available. A group attempting to do so would not need to establish a massive undertaking like the Manhattan Project.

In 1977, a student studying physics at Princeton University in new Jersey set out to design a plutonium bomb as his thesis project. Within five months he had successfully done so. All of the necessary information was easy to find. Today, with the help of the Internet, it would be possible for someone with the right scientific background to design a working nuclear bomb.

The real difficulty is not the technical know-how, but getting hold of the right kind of fuel. Nuclear fuel, known as fissile material, must be very pure to be capable of producing a nuclear explosion. Fissile material that is pure enough to use in a bomb is referred to as weapons-grade uranium, or plutonium. Nuclear power stations do not need this kind of fissile material to produce electricity for peaceful purposes. There is therefore little reason for a country to seek such material unless it is trying to manufacture a nuclear weapon.

Opposite: The final stage of uranium enrichment produces a solid mass of uranium-235 like the one shown here. The metal disc weighs nearly 10 pounds (4.5 kg) and is suitable for use in a nuclear weapon.

FISSILE MATERIAL

Fissile material is needed to power a nuclear explosion. Elaborate processes are used to produce the two fissile materials used in nuclear weapons, uranium-235 and plutonium-239. Uranium-235 makes up only 1 percent of natural uranium deposits. It has to be separated from the more common form, uranium-238, using a process called enrichment. The finished product, called highly enriched uranium (HEU), contains at least 20 percent uranium-235. Plutonium-239 does not exist naturally. It is produced in nuclear power plants, which have reactors fueled with uranium-238. During the reactor's operation, the uranium-238 absorbs an extra particle called a neutron and becomes plutonium-239.

At a hearing of the House Armed Services Committee in Washington D.C., military adviser Peter Pry shows what a "suitcase" nuclear weapon might look like.

Fortunately, weapons-grade fissile material is hard to come by. It does not occur in nature and can only be produced by a complex process. Special facilities are needed to turn uranium mined from Earth into highly enriched uranium (HEU), suitable for weapons, or for reprocessing used nuclear reactor fuel into weapons-grade plutonium. The facilities needed are prominent and visible structures. Their presence in a country that is not supposed to be producing fissile material will immediately make IAEA inspectors suspicious.

Buying or Stealing Nuclear Material

Because nuclear know-how is not hard to obtain, it is vital that weapons-grade fuel should not fall into the wrong hands. Without fissile material, or any way to produce it, it is impossible to build a nuclear weapon. With the fissile material, it is frighteningly easy. A rogue government or terrorist group could obtain the material either by stealing it or by buying it illegally on the black market.

An even more frightening situation would arise if criminals managed to steal or buy an operational nuclear weapon. Someone with almost no expertise could carry out a nuclear attack with a functioning nuclear weapon.

Such fears have intensified since the end of the Cold War. The breakup of the Soviet Union raised concerns about the fate of that formerly powerful country's nuclear arsenal and stocks of fissile materials. Observers feared that groups within the Soviet military might sell off nuclear weapons to the highest bidder. No one can be entirely sure that all the weapons of the Soviet era were accounted for. Up to 100 small nuclear bombs, designed to be used by spies behind enemy lines in the event of war, were rumored to be missing. Those weapons are often referred to as "suitcase" nukes because they are small enough to fit inside a suitcase or backpack. They would be ideally suited for a terrorist planning a sneak attack.

RESEARCH REACTORS

During the Cold War, the United States and the Soviet Union helped many countries build research reactors. Those are used for scientific work and research. There are now at least 130 research reactors, some containing uranium pure enough to be used in a nuclear weapon. Many reactors are in countries that are too poor to keep them fully secure. In 1997, criminals stole highly enriched uranium from a reactor in the African nation of Zaire (now Democratic Republic of the Congo) and sold it on the black market. Police eventually tracked down the material in Italy. The U.S. Department of Energy is a leading player in the ongoing international effort to recover vulnerable material and to secure reactors. Specialists can modify reactors to run on low-enriched uranium (LEU), which cannot be used in weapons manufacture.

To add to the problems, Soviet nuclear weapons were stationed on the territories of several of its former republics, now independent states. In the 1990s, the United States organized the Cooperative Threat Reduction (CTR) Program. It aimed to return the nuclear warheads in Kazakhstan, Ukraine, and Belarus to Russia. The CTR also set up a long-term program to decommission, or put out of use, launch sites and other nuclear facilities in the three republics.

Measures to safeguard nuclear weapons and fissile material within Russia itself were notoriously poor. The country went through a difficult period during the 1990s, and many sensitive sites were left underprotected or even unguarded. Security personnel were commonly underpaid. That raised concerns that they might be tempted to sell the weapons or help people steal them in exchange for money. Inspectors of Russian sites have repeatedly criticized the minimal security precautions taken. Although the Russian government's control over its nuclear infrastructure has improved in the 2000s, some experts claim that many sites are still vulnerable.

Smuggling Nuclear Material

Fissile material is an attractive target for thieves because there are nations and terrorist groups willing to pay a great deal of money for it. Between 1993 and 2005, the IAEA recorded 220 attempts to smuggle nuclear material across national borders. The thieves have often been caught in the act or captured in another country with stolen fissile material. However, those are only the cases that have been discovered. A successful smuggling operation would probably not be exposed until someone noticed what had been stolen. In 1997, a Russian inspection of a site in Georgia, a former Soviet state, found that a significant amount of highly enriched uranium weighing at least 2 pounds (0.9 kg) was missing. Some sites are inspected so rarely that such thefts might not be discovered for years.

The punishments for nuclear smuggling are often surprisingly lenient. The courts in countries where smugglers are captured frequently sentence them to only about two years in prison. Some

A security guard in Uzbekistan scans a vehicle with a radiation monitor. The United States provided funding for detection equipment in some former Soviet states, hoping to reduce the threat of nuclear smuggling out of the region.

observers argue that the arms control and smuggling laws under which nuclear thieves are prosecuted are inadequate. They suggest that more severe laws are needed to deal with nuclear smugglers.

Abdul Qadeer Khan's Nuclear Network

Criminals smuggle nuclear material to make money. They sell the materials to governments that wish to develop nuclear weapons or to increase their existing arsenals. Some countries sell the material themselves. The Pakistani scientist Dr. Abdul Qadeer Khan ran a particularly infamous network. It sold the technologies needed to purify fissile material into a form suitable for weapons.

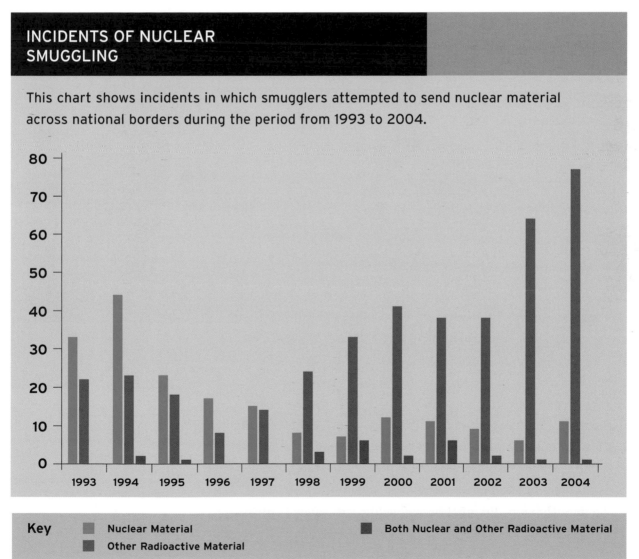

INCIDENTS OF NUCLEAR SMUGGLING

This chart shows incidents in which smugglers attempted to send nuclear material across national borders during the period from 1993 to 2004.

Key
- Nuclear Material
- Other Radioactive Material
- Both Nuclear and Other Radioactive Material

Source: International Atomic Energy Agency

ABDUL QADEER KHAN

Dr. Abdul Qadeer Khan (1936–) is a Pakistani scientist who has been called the "father of the Islamic bomb." His role as the founder and mastermind of Pakistan's nuclear weapons program made him a national hero. He later became notorious for his role in the proliferation of nuclear weapons technology. In 2003, reports emerged that Pakistan had supplied components for uranium enrichment to Iran and Libya. Khan confessed that he had sold nuclear technology. He claimed he had acted without the knowledge of the Pakistani government. He has since withdrawn his confession, claiming that the government was well aware of his activities.

Though officially disgraced, Abdul Qadeer Khan remains a hero to many Pakistanis as the creator of their country's nuclear weapons program. Here, supporters wave Khan's portrait during a 2007 march celebrating the anniversary of Pakistan's first successful nuclear test.

In 1998, under Khan's guidance, Pakistan succeeded in testing a nuclear weapon. It became the first Islamic state to enrich weapons-grade uramium. Initially, experts were most worried about the possibility of a nuclear conflict between Pakistan and its nuclear-armed neighbor, India. However, that anxiety was soon overtaken by another fear. On September 11, 2001, the Islamist terrorist network al-Qaeda used hijacked planes as missiles to attack the United States. Many people feared that religious extremists within Pakistan might pass nuclear information and material to terrorists planning future attacks.

The nuclear network set up by Khan seems to have been motivated by profit rather than ideals. He sold parts and plans for nuclear techology to countries with very different political systems and religious beliefs. His customers included Iran, Libya, and North Korea. The IAEA described Khan's network as "a Wal-Mart of private sector proliferation." His operation did not make much effort to keep its activities secret. The information Khan distributed had a picture of his own face superimposed on the mushroom cloud of a nuclear explosion. Some experts believe Khan's claims that the government of Pakistan was involved in his schemes.

WHAT WOULD YOU DO?

You Are in Charge

You are an adviser working for the energy department. Your country uses nuclear energy to generate much of its electricity. You have been asked to research the risks posed by nuclear smuggling. You must suggest how the government should spend its budget most efficiently to reduce that threat. What will you propose? Why?

- Improve border policing to make sure that no radioactive material is smuggled out of your country.
- Convert research reactors to run on nuclear fuels that are not suitable for use in weapons.
- Offer financial aid to foreign governments to help them guard their nuclear sites.

CHAPTER 5

Nuclear Attack

It is 2025. Elise and her family cannot leave their home. Terrorists have detonated a weapon called a "dirty bomb" on the city's subway. That kind of weapon uses explosives to spread hazardous radioactive material. The city authorities have instructed everyone to remain indoors while scientists measure the extent of the radioactive contamination. Although Elise lives far from the location of the attack, she will still be affected by it. She knows that the subway will be closed for a long time. She and thousands of others will have to find other ways to travel in a city where the roads are already extremely congested. That will make it harder for the city's inhabitants to work and prosper. Elise is afraid that even more damaging attacks may follow in the future.

New Threats

Nuclear weapons and their proliferation remain a very real threat to the modern world. Many experts think a nuclear incident is highly likely in the future. A report by the U.S. Senate Foreign Relations Committee in 2005 took the bleak view that there was a 29 percent likelihood of a nuclear strike on American soil by 2015.

The current climate is very different from that of the Cold War. That superpower rivalry was frightening, but the two sides developed codes and rules that helped maintain peace. After the Cuban Missile Crisis, a permanent telephone hotline, known as the "red" telephone, allowed the U.S. president and the Soviet leader to contact each other immediately in the event of a crisis. During the 1970s, arms control negotiations ensured that talks between the two sides would go on continuously.

DIRTY BOMBS

A "dirty bomb" is the common name for a radiological weapon. It is a conventional bomb packed with radioactive material, which scatters when the bomb goes off. Dirty bombs are not true nuclear bombs. There is no nuclear chain reaction and therefore no enormous explosion. Dirty bombs are designed instead to disperse radiation over as wide an area as possible. Terrorists could make a dirty bomb by using commonly found radioactive isotopes such as caesium, which is used in radiation therapy for cancer patients.

CURRENT NUCLEAR ARSENALS

These are the estimated world nuclear arsenals in 2008:

Country	Estimated number of nuclear weapons
North Korea	12
India	50
Pakistan	70
Israel	200
United Kingdom	200
China	320
France	350
United States	5,736
Russia	7,200

Source: Center for Defense Information

People have dreaded the possibility of a nuclear attack since the 1950s. In the United States, many families installed their own bomb shelters, stocked with canned food, in which to take refuge if a nuclear war ever broke out.

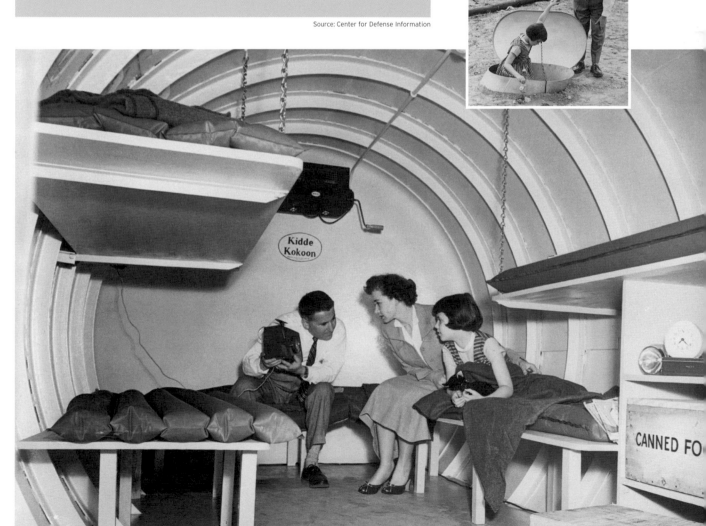

While the United States and the Soviet Union had very different political systems and beliefs, both were motivated by national and material interests and, on the whole, behaved rationally. Neither desired their own destruction. In the contemporary world, the strategy of deterrence may no longer prove as effective.

With the rise of terrorism, enemies are harder to identify. The behavior of terrorists is neither rational nor predictable. Suicide bombers, for example, seem driven by a wish to destroy that is stronger than any concern for their own lives. That makes them extremely hard to defend against. One of the great fears of the current world is that such people might obtain nuclear weapons.

NUCLEAR TERRORISM IN FICTION

There have been several fictional portrayals of nuclear terrorism. A well-known example was the 1991 novel *The Sum of All Fears*, by Tom Clancy, in which terrorists plan to detonate a nuclear weapon at an American Super Bowl. In the sixth season of the Fox television drama *24*, terrorists succeed in detonating a nuclear device in Los Angeles, California. And the 2005 HBO movie *A Dirty War* depicted the impact of a dirty bomb attack in London.

Disaster Scenario: Nuclear Terrorism

For many people, the threat of nuclear weapons has taken on a new urgency since the events of September 11, 2001. The 9/11 attacks were planned by the Islamist terrorist network al-Qaeda. The terrorists hijacked four planes, intending to crash them into major targets within the United States. They crashed two of the planes into the twin towers of the World Trade Center in New York City, and a third into the Pentagon in Virginia, which houses the U.S. Department of Defense. Passengers on the fourth plane attempted to overpower the hijackers. Those terrorists — probably realizing they

were going to lose control of the plane — crashed it in a field in Pennsylvania without reaching their target, possibly the U.S. Capitol in Washington, D.C.

The attack demonstrated what an organized terrorist group eager to kill on a grand scale could achieve, especially if its members were prepared to die. If fanatical terrorists like those could obtain the right materials from the black market and gain the assistance of sympathetic scientists, the nightmare of a terrorist nuclear weapon could become a reality.

Firefighters make their way through the rubble following the 9/11 attack on the World Trade Center. Their heroic efforts to save people cost many New York firefighters their lives.

Disaster Scenario: Nuclear War

Despite the collapse of the Soviet Union and the end of the Cold War, the United States and Russia remain prepared for a nuclear conflict with each other. Old habits die hard, and the United States continues to rehearse large-scale military operations in which Russia is the opponent in a nuclear war. On the Russian side, scientists continue to improve the country's missiles, with the aim of ensuring that Russian nuclear weapons could penetrate any U.S. anti-ballistic missile system.

Nonetheless, a war between the old enemies is currently unlikely. Nuclear-tipped ballistic missiles are more likely to be used in other conflicts. For example, China is engaged in a long-term dispute with the island of Taiwan, which it regards as a rebel province and refuses to recognize as an independent nation. In a nightmare scenario, China might use its nuclear weapons against Taiwan, prompting a nuclear response against China by the West. Any such war would involve nuclear weapons far more powerful than the bombs dropped on Japan in 1945.

Disaster Scenario: Concealed Nuclear Device

A disturbing fact about nuclear weapons is that they are extremely hard to detect. Instruments cannot easily distinguish between background radiation, which is present everywhere, and a bomb with a uranium core. The latest scanners are better than ever at identifying different types of radiation, but those have quite a short range. The danger therefore remains that devices will be smuggled across national borders undetected.

Fewer than 5 percent of cargo containers entering the United States are opened and inspected by customs officers. Many illegal items, such as drugs, are smuggled into the United States by sea, passing through the ports in containers. Using such methods, a terrorist group or a hostile government

ATOMIC DETECTIVES

In 1974, hoaxers claimed to have placed a nuclear bomb in the city of Boston and threatened to detonate it. In response to the incident, then President Gerald Ford established Nuclear Emergency Support Teams (NEST). The NEST teams are made up of expert volunteers. They are sent with scanning equipment to investigate potential nuclear threats. Because they often travel in disguise, they are sometimes called "nuclear ninjas."

could smuggle a nuclear bomb into the United States or some other country to carry out a surprise attack.

Disaster Scenario: Attack on a Nuclear Power Station

If would-be attackers could not obtain a nuclear weapon of their own, they might decide to target a nuclear power plant instead. The 1986 accident at the civilian reactor at Chernobyl in the Ukraine (then part of the Soviet Union) contaminated a wide area. A similar result could be achieved deliberately by terrorists if they managed to damage a nuclear reactor.

An explosion takes place at a mock nuclear facility in Nevada as part of a training exercise. The site is used to train emergency response personnel.

In order to spread radiation from the reactor, attackers would have to penetrate the nuclear power plant's containment building. That is a solidly-built, airtight structure designed to keep radiation inside in the event of a meltdown. A meltdown occurs if the nuclear fuel in the reactor core overheats. The use of planes as offensive weapons in the 9/11 attacks prompted experts to wonder whether a plane intentionally crashed into a reactor could release radiation into the environment.

Another target at a power plant could be the pool of water used to cool down fuel rods that are no longer in use. Those rods are highly radioactive and extremely hot. The cold water prevents them from melting and releasing their radiation into the environment. If terrorists were somehow able to drain the pool, the rods would melt and give off large quantities of harmful radiation.

Firefighters in Seattle, Washington, take part in a 2003 simulation of a dirty bomb attack. They wear anti-contamination suits to protect them from radiation.

DIRTY BOMB IN MOSCOW

On November 23, 1995, a dirty bomb containing the radioisotope caesium-137 and a mixture of explosives was discovered in Ismailovsky Park in Moscow, Russia. It had been placed there by a terrorist group fighting for Chechen independence from Russia. The Chechens decided not to detonate the weapon but to gain publicity for their cause by telling television journalists where it was. Although no harm was done, the incident highlighted the potential danger of a terrorist attack using a dirty bomb.

After 9/11, the U.S. Nuclear Regulatory Commission (NRC) admitted that none of the 103 reactors in the United States had been designed to withstand the impact of a jetliner. However, since the attacks, the NRC has studied the problem and worked to improve the defenses of U.S. nuclear plants. Their studies found it unlikely that a plane could cause damage serious enough to release large quantities of radiation.

Disaster Scenario: Dirty Bomb

Experts agree that it would be extremely difficult to cause mass casualties with a dirty bomb attack. However, a dirty bomb could cause widespread panic and disruption. It could also contaminate a large area for a long time, requiring the evacuation of the population and bringing businesses and transportation systems to a halt.

WHAT WOULD YOU DO?

You Are in Charge

You are a member of the United Nations Terrorism Prevention Branch. You are in talks with representatives of various nations, discussing the best ways to prevent a nuclear terrorist attack. The representatives are urging the development of new technologies to detect the radioactive cores of nuclear weapons. Current technologies require close-range scans to detect possible threats and are not very effective. What do you propose?

- You agree with their focus on new technologies. We need to be able to find and disarm nuclear weapons if they are smuggled into our cities.

- You argue that money would be better spent on increasing security at ports and airports. Manually checking baggage and freight would be effective and could be done immediately.

CHAPTER 6

Meeting the Challenge

It is 2025. Sarah is an expert on international relations and non-proliferation. She heads a team that has been asked to work on new approaches to halting proliferation. Recent threats from rogue nations and terrorist groups have forced the international community to act more aggressively. Security at nuclear installations has already been strengthened. Sarah's team has just completed a report suggesting new safety measures be taken. It has been well received by the United Nations. The report recommends a system of consistent and fair penalties for nations that do not comply with international inspections. Sarah is optimistic that the world will soon agree on a united approach to reducing the threat of nuclear proliferation.

Diffusing the Situation

The Nuclear Non-Proliferation Treaty that came into force in 1970 has had some success. The most striking achievement involved South Africa. During the 1970s, South Africa developed nuclear weapons. However, in 1992 it became the first country in history to give up its nuclear arsenal. South Africa signed the Non-Proliferation Treaty and allowed IAEA inspectors into the country to dismantle the existing weapons.

The Non-Proliferation Treaty has also made it more difficult for other nations to develop nuclear weapons. Treaty members are forbidden to export materials and technology for nuclear weapons. Aspiring nuclear nations are forced to turn to the black market. IAEA inspectors, provided they can get access, can detect nuclear weapons programs before they are completed.

Even so, the Non-Proliferation Treaty's success has been limited. Current nuclear-armed nations show no sign of giving up their weapons. Most significantly, there are now more countries that posess nuclear weapons

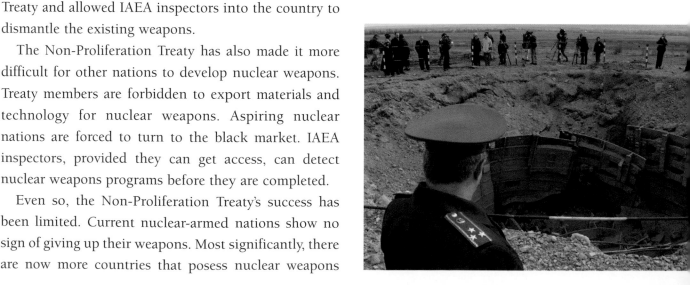

A Ukrainian officer surveys a decommissioned missile silo on October 30, 2001. That day Ukraine destroyed the last of its ICBM silos as part of a U.S.-funded plan to make it into a non-nuclear-armed state.

than there were in 1970. Information on how to construct nuclear bombs is readily available. Some of the vital fissile material that could be used to construct a weapon is not well guarded. Some completed weapons built during the Cold War may be stored insecurely. Others may have disappeared, perhaps finding their way to dangerous organizations or regimes. Consequently, the international community is faced with difficult challenges to track and secure nuclear material.

Securing Fissile Material

Keeping fissile material out of the wrong hands requires a determined effort. The Cooperative Threat Reduction Program (CTR) is an important step in this direction. The CTR was set up in 1991 by Senator Richard G. Lugar (Republican, Indiana) and former Georgia Democratic Senator Sam Nunn. It aims to dismantle weapons in the former Soviet Union. The CTR project continues to help dispose of old weapons, dismantling sites, and securing nuclear materials.

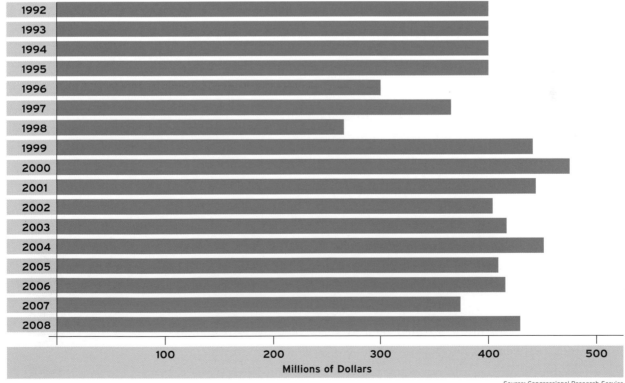

U.S. Funding for the Cooperative Threat Reduction Program

Millions of Dollars

Source: Congressional Research Service

Many experts, including Nunn and Mohamed ElBaradei, director general of the IAEA, have called for greater international oversight of fissile material production. They believe that the international community as a whole should monitor the production of nuclear fuel. That would allow greater openness and scrutiny. It would also reduce the opportunities for black market operations and make it harder to secretly produce weapons-grade materials.

Non-Proliferation Diplomacy: Iran

The Middle Eastern country of Iran is at the center of a proliferation crisis. In 2006, Iran succeeded in enriching uranium. Uranium enrichment was not a breach of the Non-Proliferation Treaty. However, many in the international community feared that Iran might go on to develop nuclear weapons. Iran insists that it does not want to develop nuclear weapons, only nuclear power. The possibility of an Iranian nuclear bomb is particularly worrying for the United States and other Western countries. Iran is ruled by an Islamist regime that has been very hostile to the West and Israel. Iran also has ties with terrorists.

Iran has insisted on continuing to enrich uranium, despite a United Nations (U.N.) Security Council resolution ordering it to stop. The U.N. has imposed economic sanctions on the country, restricting its trade as well as offering incentives. However, those measures have not persuaded Iran to stop its program. In June 2008, the five permanent members of the U.N. Security Council (the United States, the United Kingdom, Russia, France, and China) offered to help Iran build two nuclear reactors and guaranteed a regular supply of nuclear fuel. Iran, however, remained defiant.

Counter-Proliferation Diplomacy: North Korea

The most recent addition to the nuclear club, North Korea, successfully performed a nuclear test in 2006. North Korea is ruled by an unpredictable dictator, Kim Jong-il, which makes its

SHUTTING DOWN THE BLACK MARKET

The nuclear black market poses a serious threat. However, determined action can bring positive results. In 2003, the United States stopped an illegal shipment of nuclear components heading for Libya, a North African country that has supported terrorism in the past. The shipment contained equipment needed to enrich uranium. It had been supplied by the nuclear network of Pakistan's Dr. Abdul Qadeer Khan. Caught red-handed, Libya admitted having a secret nuclear weapons program, and Libya agreed to honor the Non-Proliferation Treaty it had signed and end its program.

possession of nuclear weapons particularly worrying. Most experts believe that North Korea's missiles lack the range to threaten the United States. However, they pose a direct threat to North Korea's neighbors in East Asia, including South Korea and Japan.

In 2003, a South Korean protester burns the North Korean flag next to a model of a nuclear missile. North Korea's nuclear program caused fear and outrage in South Korea.

The international community has made strong diplomatic efforts to persuade North Korea to dismantle its nuclear weapons program. Hopes for a solution rest on the long-running Six-Party Talks involving North Korea, China, South Korea, the United States, Russia, and Japan.

There is no immediate prospect of the North Koreans giving up their weapons. However, negotiations have made some progress toward halting the country's production of additional nuclear material. In October 2008, North Korea agreed to U.S. demands to halt plutonium production and allow inspectors to visit its nuclear sites. In return, the U.S. State Department removed North Korea from its list of state sponsors of terrorism. Some critics feel that the agreement is inadequate, because North Korea may have secret nuclear sites. North Korea also suffers from regular shortages of food and electricity. Those conditions may eventually persuade it to give up its nuclear weapons in exchange for foreign aid and an end to economic sanctions.

The Military Option

When politicians lose patience with diplomacy, they often turn to military action. Following the 9/11 attacks, the United States and its allies engaged in a number of military operations. A U.S.-led coalition invaded Afghanistan, where the ruling Taliban were sheltering al-Qaeda terrorists. When intelligence agents explored deserted al-Qaeda camps in Afghanistan, they found diagrams showing how to make nuclear weapons. That discovery fueled Western fears that a terrorist organization might link up with a rogue nation to acquire and master nuclear technology.

In 2003, the United States and its allies undertook another military intervention, invading Iraq. They toppled the Iraqi dictator Saddam Hussein, who was suspected of trying to develop nuclear or other weapons of mass destruction. It turned out that Hussein had not been able to fully develop such programs, and the war has since been widely criticized. However, many governments continue to view military force as a necessary option, particularly in cases where nuclear arms or other weapons of mass destruction pose a direct threat to world peace and security.

Opposite: **This satellite photograph shows a site in Syria that was bombed by Israeli planes in 2007. The Israelis claimed that it was a nuclear facility, part of a secret Syrian nuclear weapons program. Syria denied that charge. Israel is determined to prevent its hostile Arab neighbors from obtaining nuclear weapons.**

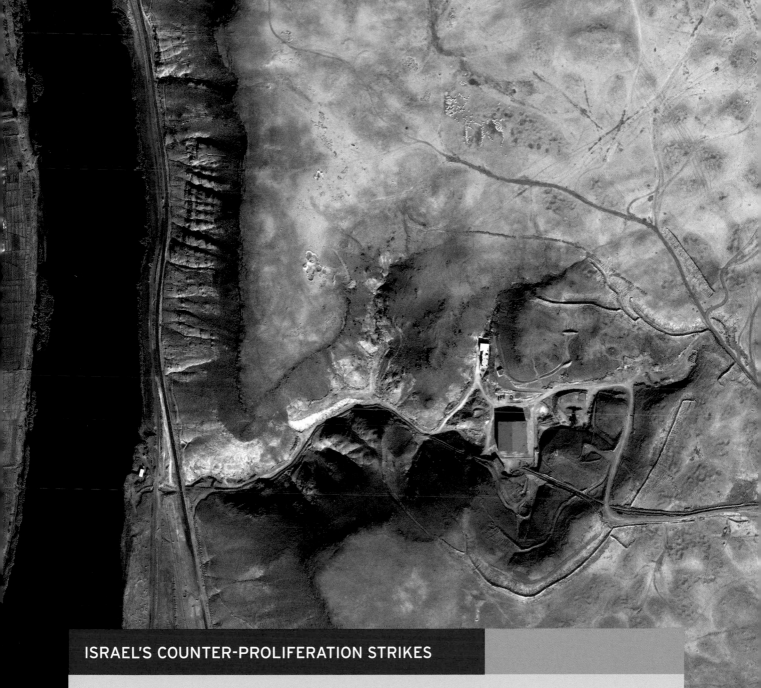

ISRAEL'S COUNTER-PROLIFERATION STRIKES

Israel is a small Jewish state in the Middle East. It is friendly with the West and is surrounded by hostile Arab neighbors. Israel has nuclear weapons of its own and has been aggressive in its efforts to prevent neighboring Arab countries from acquiring them. Israel's actions may have helped prevent nuclear proliferation, although its motive was simply self-defense.

- On June 7, 1981, Israel carried out an air strike against an Iraqi nuclear reactor. The Israelis claimed that Iraq planned to use the reactor to produce nuclear weapons, which could be used against Israel.

- On September 6, 2007, Israel bombed a site in Syria. The Israelis claimed that the site held a reactor capable of producing plutonium-239 for nuclear weapons.

THE COMPREHENSIVE TEST BAN TREATY

In 1996, a new international treaty, the Comprehensive Test Ban Treaty (CTBT), was proposed. That treaty banned all nuclear tests, improving on the Partial Test Ban Treaty of 1963, which permitted underground tests (see page 15). By 2008, the CTBT had been signed by 180 countries. However, the treaty is still not in force. It cannot go into effect until certain key, nuclear-armed countries have formally approved it. So far, not all of them are willing to do so. The countries that have not yet signed the treaty include Pakistan, India, North Korea, and the United States.

Survivors of the 1945 nuclear strike on Hiroshima remember the victims of that attack. They are burning incense and offering prayers at Peace Memorial Park in Hiroshima, Japan, on the 63rd anniversary of the bombing in 2008.

Moving Toward Disarmament

For as long as nuclear weapons have existed there have been calls for them to be abolished. In the modern world, with its nine nuclear-armed nations, the goal of total disarmament seems further away than ever. Those that have nuclear weapons are unwilling to give them up while others remain armed. They also enjoy the power that comes with having a nuclear arsenal.

A world free of nuclear weapons may become a reality one day. However, the immediate task is to stop their proliferation. Reducing stockpiles of weapons would be an important step toward limiting the danger of an accidental nuclear detonation. The global community must be ready to help countries that have difficulties safeguarding their nuclear material. All nations must take care to prevent unauthorized nuclear traffic across their borders.

Regular inspections and improved technology should ensure that nations cannot produce the material they need to develop nuclear bombs. Internationally approved and enforced penalties would help deter both would-be suppliers of nuclear materials and countries tempted to develop nuclear weapons. A consistent approach, backed by the entire international community, seems the only hope of tackling and reversing proliferation.

By shrinking their own arsenals, the nuclear nations could set an example to the rest of the world. If countries that have nuclear weapons refuse to give them up, convincing other countries not to develop them remains an uphill battle. Everyone fears a nuclear attack. As long as having nuclear weapons is seen as a deterrent to nuclear attack, other nations will continue to develop them in self-defense. Nuclear proliferation poses a grave threat to the future of the world. If we do nothing, there may not be a safe future.

WHAT WOULD YOU DO?

You Are in Charge

You are a member of the United Nations. Reliable intelligence suggests that an aggressive power has a secret nuclear weapons program. No one can agree on what should be done. Some favor a military invasion to remove the aggressive regime from power. Others prefer to impose economic sanctions until IAEA inspectors are allowed into the country. Which approach will you advocate? Why?

- Economic sanctions, diplomacy, and inspections are the best solution because an invasion is likely to be costly in lives and resources.

- Invasion is the best solution because economic sanctions work very slowly if at all. The aggressive power must not be given time to develop a nuclear weapon.

Glossary

al-Qaeda An Islamist terrorist network led by Saudi Arabian Osama bin Laden and believed to have been responsible for the 9/11 attacks

atom The smallest unit of matter that is identifiable as a specific chemical element

black market An illegal market where stolen or illicit items are bought and sold

blockade An action that prevents supplies from reaching a country

Cold War The worldwide struggle for power and influence between the United States and the Soviet Union, together with their respective allies, which lasted from 1945 to 1990

communist A member of a political system who believes the state should have total control over wealth and property

deterrence A strategy of discouraging enemy attack by maintaining sufficient military force to retaliate

fallout Radioactive contamination left behind by a nuclear explosion

fissile material Radioactive material suitable for creating a nuclear reaction

highly enriched uranium (HEU) Uranium that has been processed to make it suitable for use in weapons

intercontinental ballistic missile (ICBM) A long-range missile used to attack distant countries. An ICBM can be fitted with a nuclear warhead.

isotope A form of an element that differs from other forms of the same element because it has a different number of neutrons. Only specific isotopes can be used as nuclear fuel.

monopoly Complete control or ownership by a single individual, organization, or country

mushroom cloud The cloud of condensed gas and debris produced by a very powerful explosion. The mushroom cloud has become a symbol of nuclear war and destruction.

Nazi regime The government of Adolf Hitler's National Socialist Party, which ruled Germany from 1933 to 1945

nuclear fission The process of splitting the nucleus of an atom to release energy

nuclear fusion The process in which the nuclei of light atoms, such as hydrogen and deuterium, combine to form a heavier nucleus, releasing energy

nucleus The cluster of particles at the center of an atom

plutonium A metallic element used in the production of nuclear weapons

radiation Energy emitted in the form of particles by substances such as uranium and plutonium, whose atoms are not stable and are spontaneously decaying

republic A state with a system of government in which supreme power is in the hands of representatives elected by the people

rogue state A term sometimes used to describe states ruled by erratic dictatorial regimes, many of which oppress their own people and sponsor terrorism

sanctions Economic measures intended to punish a state or make it change its policies. For example, another country or an international organization may cease trading with the target state.

smuggling Illegally bringing something across a national border

Soviet Union Also known as the U.S.S.R. (Union of Soviet Socialist Republics), a country consisting of Russia and a number of other East European, Baltic, and Central Asian states. The leading communist power, the Soviet Union, existed from 1922 to 1991.

superpower A term used during the Cold War to describe the United States and the Soviet Union; the United States is now regarded as the sole superpower

United Nations An international organization, created in 1945 to foster cooperation, friendship, and peace between nations

uranium A metallic element used in the manufacture of nuclear weapons

weapons of mass destruction (WMD) Nuclear, chemical, or biological weapons that are designed to kill and destroy on a very large scale

Further Information

Books

Harris, Nathaniel. *Witness to History: Hiroshima* (Heinemann, 2004)

Minneus, Steve. *In the News: Nukes: The Spread of Nuclear Weapons* (Rosen Publishing Group, 2007)

Olwell, Russell B. *Global Organizations: The International Atomic Energy Agency* (Chelsea House Publishers, 2008)

Phillips, Tracey A. *Issues in Focus Today: Weapons of Mass Destruction: The Threat of Chemical, Biological and Nuclear Weapons* (Enslow, 2007)

Web Sites

Eyewitness to History: Hiroshima
www.eyewitnesstohistory.com/hiroshima.htm
Read primary source accounts of people who witnessed the nuclear bombing of Hiroshima during World War II.

Nuclear Terrorism FAQs
www.nuclearterrorism.org/faq.html
Review answers to frequently asked questions about the possibility of a nuclear terror attack. Applications include "Blast Maps," which visualizes the consequences a nuclear strike.

ThinkQuest.org
library.thinkquest.org/17940/texts/fission/fission.html
Examine the animated sequence on this web site for an inside look at a nuclear fission chain reaction.

U.S. Nuclear Regulatory Commission
www.nrc.gov/reading-rm/basic-ref/students.html
The U.S. Nuclear Regulatory Commission's Web site introduces basic facts about nuclear power, reactors, radiation, disaster prevention, and more.

What Would You Do?

Page 9:
A strong case can be made against a country keeping its nuclear weapons. Many believe that their destructive power is so great that they should never be used in any circumstances. Organizations like Greenpeace, the Sierra Club, the Nuclear Control Institute, the Institute for Energy and Environmental Research (IEER), and Physicians for Social Responsibility urge the government to give up its nuclear weapons regardless of what anyone else does. They argue that somebody must take the lead, or sooner or later, an accident or conflict will trigger a nuclear war. On the other hand, a nation that sheds its weapons leaves itself vulnerable to attack by nuclear-armed powers. It may find itself threatened, bullied, or even invaded by an aggressive regime. Should a country take the lead in disarming, or could progress be made through small, simultaneous reductions on all sides? There are no "right" answers to questions such as these.

Page 17:
Other nations will understandably fear that your country's acquisition of nuclear weapons will add to the tensions in the region. It would probably be better not to argue about the possibility of a nuclear war. Other nations will be concerned about the damage inflicted on both sides, but they will also worry about the effects of radioactive fallout on the environment both globally and within their own territories. It might be better to argue that the possession of nuclear weapons by both sides is more likely to preserve peace. That, after all, is the basis of deterrence, which many believe prevented a war between the United States and the Soviet Union during the Cold War. Neither argument is likely to convince the international community, which aims to halt nuclear proliferation.

Page 21:
Legitimate arguments can be made against nuclear power. For example, it is extremely difficult to dispose of radioactive nuclear waste. However, the fact that a country develops nuclear energy does not necessarily mean it will be able to go on from there to create nuclear weapons. An effective IAEA inspection program coupled with a coordinated international system of penalties should be able to prevent this from happening.

Page 29:
Fissile materials are essential to the manufacture of nuclear weapons, so it is vital to store such materials securely. Strengthening checks at international borders will certainly improve success rates against smuggling. Yet however diligent the checks, it will never be possible to catch every smuggler. For that reason, preventing smugglers from getting the fissile material in the first place should be the top priority. Greater international cooperation would be very helpful in the fight against nuclear smuggling. A united effort could be made to secure and track fissile materials, and all nations could agree to impose tough penalties on nuclear smugglers.

Page 37:
New technologies would be a great asset in improving the detection of nuclear weapons. However, they take time to develop, and the threat of nuclear terrorism is imminent. At present, an unknown amount of fissile material is unaccounted for. Even more seriously, complete nuclear weapons from the former Soviet Union may have gone missing. No one can be certain if and when terrorists might get their hands on a nuclear weapon. Therefore the priority should be to increase border security. Of course, countries that can afford it should also invest in the development of more sensitive radiation-scanning devices.

Page 45:
Diplomatic and economic pressure is always preferable to military action. However, many would argue that military action is sometimes necessary when dealing with an aggressive or unstable regime. If such a regime looks likely to acquire nuclear weapons, the international community must then debate the pros and cons of military action. Much will depend on intelligence estimates of how close the regime is to completing its weapons program. If the weapons are almost ready, a swift military strike against suspected weapons sites may be the safest action. But can intelligence estimates be trusted? When deciding to act, one should also consider the record of the regime: Has it repeatedly tried to develop nuclear or other weapons of mass destruction? If the weapons program is not advanced, it may be best to apply diplomatic pressure followed by economic sanctions and, later, offers of economic aid.

Index

Page numbers in **bold** refer to illustrations and charts.

About the Author

Joseph Harris was born in Kendal, Cumbria, United Kingdom. He did post-graduate research before becoming a freelance writer. He currently writes books for young people on modern history, including *Dates of a Decade: The 1980s* (Watts, 2009).